The A to Z

Farm Joke Book

From **Acorn** to **Zebra**!

Illustrated by Vasco Icuza

Kane Miller
A DIVISION OF EDC PUBLISHING

The A to Z FARM Joke Book

If you're hog wild about jokes,
and love nothing more than making others laugh,
then this is the perfect book for you!

The A to Z Farm Joke Book is a rollicking collection
of over 300 farm-themed one-liners. The jokes
are ordered alphabetically, so you can chuckle
your way from A to Z, or search for a joke about
your favorite farm animal. From amusing alpacas
to a zany zebra, the laughs don't stop!

The A to Z Farm Joke Book is all you need
to harvest a talent for joke telling!

A

Q How did the farmer explain what an **ACORN** is?

A "It's an oak tree, in a nutshell!"

HA HA!

Q Did you hear about the happy farmer who bought 100 **ACRES**?

A Now he's a Jolly Rancher!

Q How do **ALPACAS** sing?

A Alpaca-pella!

Q Which kind of **ANT** doesn't belong on an ant farm?

A Elephants!

Q What's the worst thing about having an **ANT FARM**?

A Finding a tractor small enough!

Q Why do **APPLE TREES** hate riddles?

A Because they're easily stumped!

LOL!

Q Did you hear about the **APPLES** that fell in love?

A They married and lived apple-ly ever after!

Q Did you hear about the farmhand who picked seven **ASPARAGUS** stalks instead of six?

A The last one was just a spare, I guess!

Q What do farmers call young **AVOCADOS**?

A Avo-kiddos!

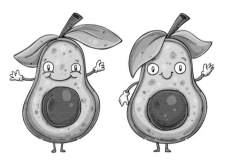

Q Why did the chicken sit on the **AXE**?

A She wanted to see if she could hatchet!

B

Q What farm animal says "**BAA** woof"?

A The sheepdog!

Q Can you name two works of literature about **BACON**?

A *Hamlet* and *Frankenswine*!

Q Why did the farmer stop making **BALES OF HAY** round?

A Because the cows needed a square meal!

Q What did the angry wheat say to the **BARLEY** in the next field?

A "Rye would you say that?"

Q How do **BARN CATS** get over a fight?

A They hiss and make up!

HAHAHA!

B

What do you call a **BARN OWL** with a low voice?

A barn growl!

Why are **BARNS** welcoming buildings?

Because they're full of "Hey!"

Why did the **BEE** go to see the farm's vet?

It had hives!

What kind of fast food is delivered to **BEEHIVES**?

Hum-burgers!

Why did the **BEEKEEPER** work so hard?

Because honey doesn't grow on trees!

HAH!

Q What happened when the farmer ate too many homegrown **BELL PEPPERS**?

A She got a bellyache!

CACKLE!

Q Which **BERRIES** taste better the older they get?

A Elderberries!

Q When should farmers buy **BIRDS**?

A When they are going cheep!

Q What do you call a truck full of **BISON**?

A A buffa-load!

Q Why did the farmer call his dog **BLACKSMITH**?

A Because every time the door was open the dog made a bolt for it!

B

Q How did the farmer make a **BLUEBERRY** turnover?

A By pushing it down a hill!

Q What do you call a **BOAR** standing at the entrance to a barn?

A A door!

Q What happens when farmers search online for something to start a **BONFIRE**?

A The search engine says "No matches found"!

Q Why did the farmers hold their **BOOTS** to their ears?

A They wanted to listen to sole music while they worked!

Q What did the **BORDER COLLIE** say when the farmer was about to trim the sheep's wool?

A "Are you shear-ious?"

HE HE!

B

Q Why do **BREAD** thieves get bad headaches?

A They have my grains!

Q Which **BREED** of cow can jump higher than a building?

A Any breed; a building can't jump!

Q What kind of music did the farmer play to help the **BROCCOLI** grow?

A Broc 'n' roll!

BWAHAHA!

Q What should you do if your cow kicks the **BUCKET** over?

A Don't cry over spilled milk, turn the udder cheek, and move on!

Q What's worse than raining **BUCKETS** on a field?

A Hailing cabs!

Q What do you call a **BUFFALO** in the chicken coop?

A Stuck!

Q What do you call a sleeping **BULL**?

A A bulldozer!

Q What do **BUNNIES** do at the farmers market?

A Shop till they hop!

Q How does a **BUNNY** keep its fur neat?

A With a hare brush!

TEE-HEE!

Q What do you call the best **BUTTER** on the farm?

A A goat!

C

What did they call the popular **CABBAGE** on the farm?

Cool Slaw!

What does a farmer call a cow with no **CALF**?

De-calf-inated!

CHORTLE!

Why did the **CALVES** love the farmer's jokes?

They enjoyed being a-moo-sed!

How do you know **CARROTS** are good for your eyes?

Because you never see a rabbit wearing glasses!

Why was the farm **CAT** afraid of the trees?

It didn't like their bark!

Q How do barn **CATS** always get the farmer to do what they want?

A They are very purr-suasive!

Q What do you call **CATTLE** with a good sense of humor?

A Laughing stock!

Q What did the **CATTLE FARMER** say when the cute calf entered the room?

A "A door, a bull!"

Q What is the difference between broccoli and **CAULIFLOWER**?

A Cauliflower is just broccoli that's seen a ghost!

Q Why was there no **CELERY** at the farmers market?

A It was out of stalk!

GIGGLE!

13

C

Q Did you hear about the dairy farmers that failed to make **CHEESE**?

A They fell at the final curdle!

SNICKER!

Q Where do they make mythical **CHEESES**?

A At the legend dairy!

Q What do you call a potato pretending to be a **CHERRY**?

A An imitator!

Q How do farmers keep a rotten **CHERRY TOMATO** from smelling?

A They pinch its nose!

Q What do you call a ghost that causes mayhem in a **CHICKEN COOP**?

A A poultry-geist!

C

Q Who tells jokes to **CHICKENS**?

A A comedi-hen!

Q What do **CHICKS** grow on?

A Eggplants!

Q How do farmers explain the difference between weather and **CLIMATE**?

A You can't weather a tree, but you can climate!

Q Why did the farmer take a **CLOCK** to the vet?

A Because it had ticks!

Q Did you hear about the farmer who built a **COMBINE HARVESTER** out of timber?

A It wooden work!

GUFFAW!

C

Q Why did the chicken **COOP** have two doors?

A Because if it had four doors, it would be a chicken sedan!

CHUCKLE!

Q How much did the pirate farmer charge for **CORN**?

A A buccaneer!

Q What do the farmer's ducks eat with their **CORN CHIPS**?

A Quack-amole!

Q Who is the highest-ranking official in a **CORNFIELD**?

A The kernel!

Q Why is **COTTON** farming like an epic film?

A Because it is the classic struggle of goods versus weevils!

C

Q How do **COTTONTAILS** travel from one farm to another?

A By hare-plane!

Q What did the farmer call the **COW** she couldn't see?

A Ca-moo-flauged!

Q Why do **COWBOYS** ride horses?

A Because they're too heavy to carry!

Q What do dairy **COWS** read in the morning?

A The moos-papers!

Q How did the cow sneak out of the **COWSHED**?

A Right pasteurize!

HAW-HAW!

17

C

Q What's the difference between a pirate and a **CRANBERRY** farmer?

A A pirate buries treasure, but a cranberry farmer treasures berries!

Q What do farmers use to make **CROP CIRCLES**?

A Protractors!

Q How do you harvest **CROPS** in the winter?

A With an ice sickle!

Q Did you hear the one about the **CROW** on the telephone pole?

A It wanted to make a long-distance caw!

Q Why was the **CUCUMBER** farmer mad?

A Because she got in a pickle!

GIGGLE!

Q What do you call a **DAIRY COW** that doesn't produce milk?

A An udder disaster!

Q What happened when two trucks crashed on the **DAIRY FARM**?

A De-brie was everywhere!

Q Do you know the joke about the **DAIRY FARMER**?

A I won't tell it to you; it's way too cheesy!

Q What do farmers who don't eat **DAIRY PRODUCTS** say when asked if they'd like a glass of milk?

A "No whey!"

Q What did the **DANDELION** say to the farmer?

A "Take me to your weeder!"

Did you hear about the **DEER FARMERS** that tried cloning?

They'd do anything to make a quick buck!

What did the farmer use to clean the **DEER'S** feet?

Hoof-paste!

What did the farmer say to the fence-post **DIGGER**?

"You're boring!"

What do you call a farm **DOG** in a cornfield?

A corn dog!

How are **DONKEYS** and turkeys similar?

They both have keys!

GUFFAW!

D

Q What's the difference between Benjamin Franklin and a **DUCK**?

A One has his face on a bill; the other has a bill on his face!

Q How do ducks leave the **DUCK HOUSE**?

A They eggs-it!

Q How does a duck swim from one side of the **DUCK POND** to the other?

A Very quack-ly!

HAH!

Q What did the **DUCKLING** detective say about the missing farmhand?

A "I've quacked the case!"

Q What do you say to the farmer who **DUG** a hole and found water?

A "Well done!"

E

What happened when the farmer mistook an **EAGLE** for a hawk?

It was hawk-ward!

TEE-HEE!

What has **EARS** but cannot hear?

A cornfield!

What do you get when a herd of cows gets caught in an **EARTHQUAKE**?

Milkshakes!

How did the chicken's **EGG** cross the road?

It scrambled across!

Why don't duck **EGGS** tell jokes?

In case they crack each other up!

E

Q Why was the bull caught on the **ELECTRIC FENCE**?

A It was charging!

Q Why couldn't the farmer drive the new **ELECTRIC TRACTOR**?

A No current license!

Q What did the **EWE** eat with her potato chips?

A Sheep dip!

Q How did the tree farmers fail their pruning **EXAM**?

A First question and they were stumped!

Q What do you call an **EXPERT** salmon farmer?

A A fish-ionado!

CACKLE!

F

Q Why shouldn't you tell secrets on a **FARM**?

A Because the potatoes have eyes, and the corn has ears!

Q What kind of **FARM ANIMAL** keeps the best time?

A A watchdog!

Q Why did the cows all shout at the **FARMER**?

A They wanted to be herd!

Q Why did the **FARMER'S DAUGHTER** study medicine?

A She wanted to go into a different field!

Q When are **FARMHANDS** cruel?

A When they pull corn by the ears!

CHORTLE!

Q What does a **FARMHOUSE** wear to a party?

A Address!

HAHAHA!

Q How did the **FARMWORKERS** get the tractor stuck?

A They drove it into a magnetic field!

Q Why didn't the farmer trust the tree in the **FARMYARD**?

A It looked pretty shady!

Q Why did the cow go through the **FENCE**?

A To get to the udder side!

Q How does **FERTILIZER** help vegetable farmers get rich?

A It raises their celery!

F

Q What grows in a **FIELD** and whispers?

A Horseradish!

HA HA!

Q How do **FLEAS** travel from one farm to another?

A By itch-hiking!

Q Why didn't the farmer cut the sheep's **FLEECE**?

A Shear laziness!

Q What do you call a **FLOCK** of young sheep tumbling down a hill?

A A lamb-slide!

Q How did the farmer perfect the **FLOWER BEDS**?

A It was a process of trowel and error!

F

Q What kind of **FLOWERS** grow under a farmer's nose?

A Tulips!

Q What do you call a **FOAL** that lives on the farm next door?

A A good neighbor!

Q Why do farmers always bump into ducks and chickens in the **FOG**?

A Because it's fowl weather!

Q What kind of dance do **FROGS** do best?

A Hip-hop!

LOL!

Q What are scarecrows' favorite **FRUIT**?

A Strawberries!

Q Why did the farmer put a trampoline in the **GARDEN** in April?

A Because it was springtime!

Q How do poultry farmers get rid of extra **GEESE**?

A They ask their neighbors to take a gander!

HA HA!

Q What is a **GOAT'S** favorite TV show?

A *America's Goat Talent!*

Q What was the **GOOSE'S** favorite city to visit?

A Honk Kong!

Q Why do farmers love jokes about **GRAINS**?

A Because they can barley control their laughter!

Q Why was the **GRASS** in the pasture so short?

A The cows were lawn moo-ers!

Q What did the **GRAZING** cows say when they walked into the meadow?

A "We've eaten herbivore!"

Q Did you hear about the **GREEN ONIONS** that started a hip-hop group?

A They called themselves the Little Rapscallions!

Q What did the flower farmer say when she **GREW** the wrong flowers?

A "Oopsie daisy!"

Q What do you call a group of **GUINEA FOWL** playing hide-and-seek?

A Fowl play!

LOL!

H

Q What did the corn farmer say after the **HARVEST**?

A "There's polenta more where that came from!"

SNICKER!

Q Why were the farmhands concerned about the combine **HARVESTER** with padded seats?

A They were worried about reaper-cushions!

Q Why is making **HAY** simple?

A It's cut and dried!

Q Did you hear about the farmer who played the bongos in a **HAYLOFT**?

A It's a drum-attic story!

Q Why did the criminal farmer sit on a **HAYSTACK**?

A He was on bale!

H

Q What happened when the **HEN** laid an egg on top of the hill?

 A She made an eggroll!

Q What did the farmer call her enormous **HENHOUSE**?

A The Eggplant!

Q What do farmers call **HENS** that can count their own eggs?

A Mathma-chickens!

Q What do farmers call an inspiring **HERB**?

A Encourage mint!

HE HE!

Q Why did the farmer stop making belts from **HERBS**?

A It was a waist of thyme!

H

How do farmers count **HERDS** of cows?

Using a cow-culator!

GIGGLE!

How long should **HIGHLAND** cattle legs be?

Long enough to touch the ground!

Why do bees stay in the **HIVE** during winter?

S'warm!

How does a **HOG** write top secret messages?

With invisible oink!

Did you know that **HOGS** dream in color?

It's a pigment of their imagination!

H

Q Did you hear about the farmer who spent the day drilling **HOLES** in metal and then bolting them together?

A At first it was boring, but then it became riveting!

Q What is a **HOLSTEIN COW'S** favorite holiday?

A Moo Year's Eve!

HA HA!

Q Did you hear about the dairy farmers who wanted to try their hand at **HONEY** farming?

A It was their plan bee!

Q What do you call a **HONEYBEE** that can't make up its mind?

A A honey maybe!

Q Why do cows have **HOOVES** rather than feet?

A Because they lactose!

H

Q What do you get when you cross a **HORSE** with strong winds?

A Tor-neigh-does!

Q Why did the **HORSE GROOMER** quit?

A He was tired of the long faces!

Q Why did the farmer put his router in with the **HORSES**?

A To get a stable connection!

Q What does it mean when you find a **HORSESHOE** in front of the stables?

A One of the horses has run off in his socks!

Q Did you hear about the **HOSE** that tried to spray the farmer in the eye?

A It completely mist!

CHUCKLE!

IJK

Q Why did the farmer call her pig "**INK**"?

A Because it was always running out of the pen!

TEE-HEE!

Q What **INSECT** ran away from the farm?

A The flea!

Q How do **JERSEY COWS** talk to one another?

A Cow-moo-nication!

Q What did the **KID** say when he woke up in a different field?

A "I have no idea how I goat here!"

Q What do barn **KITTENS** wear?

A Dia-purrs!

L

Q Why did the ducks go after the sheepdog when it swam in the **LAKE**?

A It was a pure-bread dog!

Q Why did the **LAMB** call the police?

A It was being fleeced!

Q How is the farmer's tidy **LAWN** chicken proof?

A It's impeccable!

Q What do you call a story about **LEAFY GREENS**?

A A fairy kale!

Q What do you get when you cross a **LEMON** farmer with a dinosaur?

A Tyranno-sourest Rex!

BWAHAHA!

Q What do you call leftover **LETTUCE**?

A The Romaine-der!

HAH!

Q What did the **LIMESTONE** say to the farmer?

A "Don't take me for granite!"

Q Where do farmers get medicine for their **LIVESTOCK**?

A From the pharmacy!

Q What did the **LLAMA** say when it was planning a picnic?

A "Alpaca lunch!"

Q What did the **LONGHORN SHEEP** say to the mosquito?

A "Baa, humbug!"

Q What do you call someone that used to love farm **MACHINERY**?

A An extractor fan!

Q What do you say to **MAIZE** farmers when they graduate from high school?

A "Corn-gratulations!"

Q Why did the farmer call his **MARE**, Mayo?

A Because mayonnaise!

Q Why did the farmer bury money in the **MEADOW**?

A To make the soil richer!

Q What kind of **MEDICINE** did the farmer use for her pig with a rash?

A Oink-ment!

CACKLE!

38

Q Why did the farmer's cat **MEOW** at the TV?

A Because the show was on paws!

Q What has only one horn but gives lots of **MILK**?

A A milk truck!

Q What do farmers talk about while **MILKING COWS**?

A Udder nonsense!

Q How can a farmer stop a **MOLE** from digging?

A Take away his shovel!

Q Why did the donkey say, "**MOO**"?

A Because it was learning another language!

HAHAHA!

Q What do farmers call a break where they eat **NECTARINES**?

A A pit stop!

Q If a farmer's horse says, "**NEIGH**," what does a knight's horse say?

A "Kneigh!"

Q What kind of bird always gets stuck in its **NEST**?

A A vel-crow!

HE HE!

Q Which horses only come out at **NIGHT**?

A Nightmares!

Q What was the vegetable farmer's favorite **NOVEL**?

A *War and Peas!*

O

Q What did the farmer do when the horses complained about their **OATS**?

SNICKER!

A Took the feedback!

Q Where do vegetable farmers send their **OFFSPRING**?

A To kinder-garden!

Q How did the pig feel after having its **OINK** removed?

A It was a little disgruntled!

Q What do you call the boss at **OLD MCDONALD'S FARM**?

A The C-I-E-I-O!

Q How does one onion propose to another **ONION**?

A With an onion ring!

O

Q What did the **ORANGE** say when the farmer asked what it was up to?

A "Nothing, I'm just looking round!"

HAW-HAW!

Q Did you hear about the farmer who tried to grow an apple **ORCHARD** without trees?

A His efforts were fruitless!

Q Did you hear about the farmer who started a boatbuilding business in an **OUTBUILDING**?

A Sails went through the roof!

Q What do vegetable farmers use to fix torn **OVERALLS**?

A Pumpkin patches!

Q Where do busy **OXEN** buy their clothes?

A Cattle-ogs!

P

Q What is brown and runs around the **PADDOCK**?

A A fence!

Q What did the farmer put in an empty **PAIL** to make it lighter?

A A flashlight!

Q Did you hear about the farmhand who thought there were 198 cows in the **PASTURE**?

LOL!

A There were 200 when she rounded them up!

Q Why is a **PEA** small and green?

A Because if it was large and red it would be a tomato!

Q What do farmers do when they grow too many **PEACHES**?

A They eat what they can, and they can what they can't!

P

Q What lives in **PEARS** and is an avid reader?

A A bookworm!

CHORTLE!

Q Where did the farmer go to buy a **PICKAXE**?

A The chopping mall!

Q What did the stop sign say to the **PICKUP TRUCK**?

A "Stop!"

Q What did the farmer say when the biggest **PIG** wouldn't fit in the pen?

A "There's more to you than meets the sty!"

Q What did the **PIGLET** do for his mom's birthday?

A Threw her a sow-prize party!

44

P

Q What happens when the farmer lets the **PIGLETS** out of their pen on the fifth month of the year?

 A May-ham!

SNICKER!

Q What do **PIGS** like to do when it's nice and sunny?

 A Go for a pig-nic!

Q Why shouldn't you believe anything you hear at the **PIGSTY**?

 A It's all hogwash!

Q Why did the farmer **PLANT** light bulbs?

 A He wanted a power plant!

Q Why did the farmer **PLOW** the field with a steamroller?

A To grow mashed potatoes!

Q Why did the farmhands give up **PLOWING** the field with forks?

A Because after hours of hard work, they had barely scratched the surface!

Q Why did the sheepdog jump into the **POND**?

A Because he wanted to chase the catfish!

HAH!

Q Why did the **PONY** have to go to the vet?

A He was a little horse!

Q Why was the **POTATO** scared of the end of the week?

A Because it was Fry-day!

Q Why do **POTATOES** always argue?

A Because they can never see eye to eye!

Q How did the **POULTRY** farmer become wealthy?

A He sold all his chicken stock!

Q What did the trees say to the farmer **PRUNING** them?

A "Eucalyptus!"

Q What do you get when you drop a **PUMPKIN**?

A Squash!

Q Why do farmers love working in the **PUMPKIN PATCH**?

A They are guaranteed a gourd time!

GUFFAW!

Q How did the farmers find their lost **PYGMY GOAT**?

A They tractor down!

BWAHAHA!

Q Why do ducks go **QUACK**?

A Because oink, bark, moo, and meow were already taken!

Q What do you call a laughing farmer on a **QUAD BIKE**?

A A Yamaha-hahahahahahahahahaha!

Q What did the **QUEEN BEE** say to the naughty bee?

A "Beehive yourself!"

Q What do you call a goat swimming really **QUICKLY** across a pond?

A A motor-goat!

Q What are the **QUIETEST** animals on a farm?

A The shhh-eep!

Q Where do farmers take their **RABBITS** when they're sick?

A To the hop-ital!

Q Why couldn't the **RADISH** finish the race?

A He was just a little beet!

Q Why did the **RAM** fall into the ditch?

A Because he didn't see the Ewe-turn!

CACKLE!

Q Why did the farmer add a **RAMP** to the front of the barn?

A Because she felt inclined!

Q Why did the farmhand leave the cattle **RANCH**?

A Because the pay was udder-ly terri-bull!

R What did the farmer call the **RED DEER** with perfect vision in one eye?

A A good-eye deer!

TEE-HEE!

R Why shouldn't you believe a **RICE FARMER'S** stories?

A There isn't a grain of truth in them!

R What do you get when you cross a **ROOSTER** and a cow?

A A cock-a-doodle-moo!

Q What should you do if you lose a **ROOT VEGETABLE**?

A Don't panic; it'll turnip!

R What did the farmer call the **RUSSET POTATO** that wore glasses?

A A spectator!

S

Q Why didn't the farmer feed the **SCARECROW**?

A Because it was already stuffed!

Q What happens when a farmer puts soil, **SEEDS**, and fertilizer on your head?

A It's annoying at first, but then it grows on you!

Q Why was the farmer so pleased with the new **SHEARS**?

A They were cutting-hedge technology!

Q What do you get when you cross a **SHEEP** with a policeman?

A A fleece officer!

Q What's another name for **SHEEP DIP**?

A Baa-th tub!

HA HA!

Q Why didn't the **SHEEPDOG** like jokes?

A She had herd them all before!

Q Why did the **SHEPHERD** fall asleep on the job?

A He was counting sheep!

Q What happens to farmers who can't tie their **SHOELACES**?

A They get sent to boot camp!

Q Why do farmers think **SHOVELS** are such a great invention?

A Because they are truly groundbreaking!

Q Why is it hard to photograph a **SILO**?

A The photos always come out grainy!

HAHAHA!

Q How do farmers get people to buy their extra **SOIL**?

A They sell it dirt cheap!

Q Why did the **SOW** turn off the TV?

A Because the show was a real boar!

Q What did the unicorn say to the **SPROUT**?

A "You no corn!"

Q Where do **STALLIONS** go when they're sick?

A The horse-pital!

LOL!

Q Why did the farmers keep finding coins during the **STORM**?

A It must have been the change in the weather!

S

Q Why did the farmers try to teach self-defense to their **STRAW**?

A They were tired of everyone hitting the hay!

Q What did the farmer say about the **STRAW HAT** with the built-in fan?

A "Wow, this really blows my mind!"

Q What's red, made of **STRAWBERRIES**, and sucks your blood?

A A jam-pire!

Q How are **SWEET POTATOES** able to get so much work done?

A Because they're not couch potatoes!

Q What do you call it when **SWINE** lose their memories?

A Ham-nesia!

HAH!

Q What has six legs, four eyes, two heads, and a **TAIL**?

A A farmer on a horse!

Q What do you call a farmer who **TENDS** to chickens?

A A chicken tender!

Q What type of **TOMATO** smells best?

A A Roma!

Q Did you hear about the farmer that ate his **TOOLS**?

A It was a gut wrenching experience!

Q What makes more noise than a **TRACTOR**?

A Two tractors!

HE HE!

Q What kind of animals do you need on a **TREE** farm?

A Lumber-yaks!

Q What type of **TREES** fit into a farmer's hand?

A Palm trees!

Q What do pigs call **TROUGHS**?

A All-you-can-eat buffets!

Q What happened when the fruit **TRUCK** spilled its cargo?

A It caused a huge traffic jam!

Q What was the **TURKEY** thankful for on Thanksgiving?

A Vegetarians!

GIGGLE!

Q How did the four farmers go out with only one **UMBRELLA** and not get wet?

A It wasn't raining!

Q What happens if you sit **UNDER** a cow?

A You get a pat on the head!

Q Why are spiders good at swimming **UNDERWATER**?

A They have webbed feet!

Q What is it called when a farmer **UNEXPECTEDLY** buys another barn cat?

A An impulse purr-chase!

Q Why were the neighboring livestock farmers being **UNFRIENDLY** to each other?

A There was some beef between them!

HA HA!

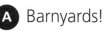

What did the **UNHAPPY** pig say to the farmer?

"You take me for grunted!"

What **UNIT** of measurement is used on farms?

Barnyards!

Where in the **UNITED STATES** can you find the most cows?

Moo York!

Why are horse-drawn carriages **UNPOPULAR** with farmers?

Because horses aren't very good at drawing!

What makes the noise of a cow when you turn it **UPSIDE DOWN**?

A cow!

CACKLE!

Q What is the fastest **VEGETABLE** on the farm?

A The runner bean!

Q Who is the smartest potato in the **VEGETABLE PATCH**?

A I yam!

Q Which new **VEGETABLES** did the farmer plant?

A Beets me!

Q What do you call a **VETERINARIAN** who specializes in canines?

A A dog-tor!

HAHAHA!

Q What are people who work in **VINEYARDS** very good at?

A Whining!

Q Why did the farmers dig a hole in a meadow and fill it with **WATER**?

A They meant well!

Q What grows when it is fed, but dies when it is **WATERED**?

A A fire!

Q What do farmers call a **WATERING CAN** with a hole in the bottom?

A A watering cannot!

Q What do you call a sheepdog that herds **WATERMELONS**?

A A melon-collie!

Q Why do well-behaved farmers refuse to walk through **WHEAT FIELDS**?

A They don't like going against the grain!

> BWAHAHA!

60

Q Why don't farmers carry four-leaf clovers in **WHEELBARROWS**?

A They don't like to push their luck!

Q Why didn't the farmer buy a machine for making **WHIPPED CREAM**?

A It felt like a big whisk!

Q What do you call a **WHITE-TAILED DEER** who can write with both hooves?

A Bambi-dextrous!

Q How many species of **WILDCATS** sneak onto farms every year?

A I don't have an exact number, but there's an ocelot of them!

Q Did you hear about the farmers who decided to grow **WILDFLOWERS**?

A They soon realized they hadn't botany!

LOL!

Q What type of music is popular on **WIND FARMS**?

A They are all big metal fans!

Q What is a **WIND TURBINE'S** favorite color?

A Blew!

Q What did the **WINDMILL** say to the famous farmer?

A "I'm a big fan!"

Q Did you hear about the farmer who hurt himself chopping **WOOD**?

A It was an axe-ident!

Q How did the first farmer discover **WOOL**?

A By shear coincidence!

CHORTLE!

Q Why did the doctor laugh at the **X-RAY** of the farmer's arm?

A It was humerus!

Q How does a **YAK** win the lottery?

A By hitting the yak-pot!

HAHAHA!

Q What do you call a stolen **YAM**?

A A hot potato!

Q What did the **YOGURT** say to the cheese at the dairy farm?

A "Ah, I see you're a man of culture as well!"

Q What happened when the farmer saw a **ZEBRA** in the stable?

A It turned out to be the horse in his pajamas!

LOL!

HA HA!

CACKLE!

BWAHAHA!

HE HE!

First American Edition 2021
Kane Miller, A Division of EDC Publishing
Copyright © Green Android Ltd 2021
Illustrated by Vasco Icuza

For information contact:
Kane Miller, A Division of EDC Publishing
5402 S 122nd E Ave
Tulsa, OK 74146
www.kanemiller.com
www.myubam.com

Library of Congress Control Number: 2021930470

Printed and bound in Malaysia, July 2021
ISBN: 978-1-68464-324-0